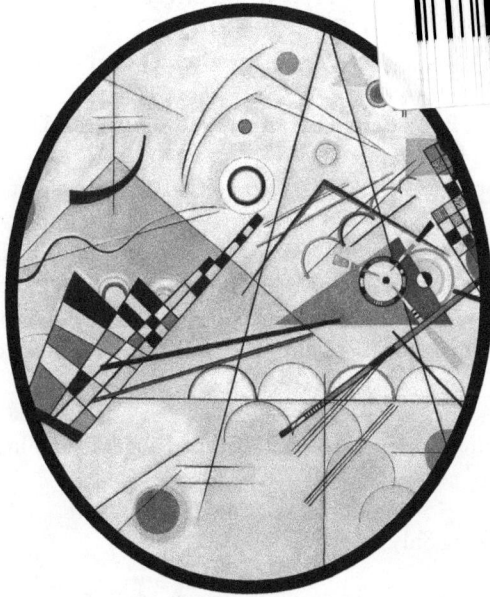

ESSAYS IN INNOVATIVE RISK MANAGEMENT METHODS

Based on Deterministic, Stochastic and Quantum Approaches

Marco Desogus and Elisa Casu

ANAPHORA LITERARY PRESS
QUANAH, TEXAS

ANAPHORA LITERARY PRESS
1108 W 3rd Street
Quanah, TX 79252
https://anaphoraliterary.com

Book design by Anna Faktorovich, Ph.D.

Printed in the United States of America, United Kingdom and in Australia on acid-free paper.

Edited by: Julie Wong Shi

Cover Image: "Composition 8" by Vasily Kandinsky. 1923. Solomon R. Guggenheim Museum, New York, Solomon R. Guggenheim Founding Collection, By gift.

JEL Codes: G32; M21; C02; E20; E51.

Published in 2018 by Anaphora Literary Press

Essays in Innovative Risk Management Methods
Marco Desogus and Elisa Casu—1st edition.

Library of Congress Control Number: 2018907298

Library Cataloging Information
Desogus, Marco, 1979-, and Casu, Elisa, 1984-, authors.
    Essays in innovative risk management methods : Based on deterministic, stochastic and quantum approaches / Marco Desogus and Elisa Casu
    62 p. ; 9 in.
    ISBN 978-1-68114-451-1 (softcover : alk. paper)
    ISBN 978-1-68114-452-8 (hardcover : alk. paper)
    ISBN 978-1-68114-453-5 (e-book)
1. Business & Economics—Banks & Banking.
2. Business & Economics—Finance—Financial Risk Management.
3. Business & Economics—Finance—Wealth Management.
HB615-715: Economic theory. Demography: Income. Factor shares:
Entrepreneurship. Risk and uncertainty.
332: Financial economics

ESSAYS IN INNOVATIVE RISK MANAGEMENT METHODS

BASED ON DETERMINISTIC, STOCHASTIC AND QUANTUM APPROACHES

Marco Desogus and Elisa Casu

CONTENTS

SYNOPSIS

This analysis works towards overcoming the current business valuation logic as prevalently set by banks and other credit entities or, more generally, within risk capital markets.

Current banking practice applies rigorous deterministic valuations that are based entirely on indices and ratios. Present accounting models are also poor representations of the correct money-credit-production-income mechanisms.

This research is structured in three chapters to propose reforms on methods of business evaluation and determining the relative solidity or probability of insolvency. Each of the themes treated has its own identity, however, they are integrated in relation to problems related to bank risk management and relevant creditworthiness assessments.

The first proposal follows the deterministic approach. Moving beyond static indicators of companies under evaluation, we look to deepen the significance of income aspects by designing mathematical measures that normalize expected flows and defining 'extended present value.'

The second chapter explores how Markov chains can contribute to understanding, evolving and improving the treatment of stochastic dynamics.

Finally, a heterodox approach to risk assessments on microcredit is offered. By applying quantum macroeconomic theory and its innovative, scientific revalations about money, output and income, we logically prove the notion that the financing of any production activity comes from the production itself. According to these assumptions, the credit that a (micro) firm benefits from originates in its own production. Therefore, the risks taken on by financial intermediaries, such as the possibility of insolvency, can be strongly reduced by reorganizing accounting systems.

1. DIAGNOSIS AND EVALUATIONS FOR PARTIAL AGGREGATES ON PRODUCT–MARKET LINES

INTRODUCTION

According to the mainstream deterministic approach in bank risk management, implementing a purely economic and financial analysis to assess company competitiveness at the aggregate level is insufficient, as strategic production, management and market choices are not directed at the aggregate.

It is therefore necessary to study diagnostic procedures in detail and to integrate further levels of partial segmentation with respect to general company production[1]. This leads to a survey of the multiple dimensions of a company's economic lines. The most basic levels of the survey, namely the single product line and the related customer segment, should therefore be considered in relation to discounted performance. Observing and understanding the practices essential to producing business results, both unitary and global, is crucial to making significant decisions about a company's competitive ability.

We work with these basal levels to investigate the potentialities of the product-market combinations. In a health scenario, strategic choices concerning production range and positioning towards customers should be weighted alongside systemic procedures, as a company reaches the market through the interdependent transversality of its overall production. During a crisis period, however, it is appropriate and necessary to conduct a relevant and targeted analysis, bearing in mind the changes in an individual unit of the business relative to those in other units. In fact, it is unrealistic to speculate customers' perfectly homogeneous behavior and inclination to purchase with respect to modifications within a company. Therefore, it is important to consider product and market evaluations through the weighting of product-market singularities, stochastic and otherwise. The phases of a product-

---

1   Cf. Damodaran (2015).

market analysis are as follows:

- identification of product-market combinations;
- allocation of economic components (costs and revenues) of each combination;
- analysis of the results.

The first phase is essential because poorly defined market combinations limit the emergence of the most important strategic relationships. There are several criteria for identifying products: they can be classified by product line, raw materials, technologies and production processes or phases of the life cycle. Similarly, markets can be segmented on a geographical basis, by distribution channel or by type of customer. The difficulties that characterize this phase of analysis arise mainly from the need to synthesize the entire product-market structure, and from the boundaries between nuanced sectors. It is therefore crucial to identify a set of combinations that are consistent with the analytical logic of the economic result achieved and that are suitable for programming and monitoring resultant behaviors. This process is based on an initial survey of the aggregate criteria so that the analysis is focused on the criteria most important for a sustainable crisis support plan. Since it involves a more complex system, this phase is delicate but significant as new relationships are often highlighted and better insight on the topic is achieved. Once the individual product-market combinations have been defined, each economic value must be recalculated according to marginalist logic and the distinction between fixed and variable costs[2]. For each singularity, we then determine three increasingly detailed configurations of the products-markets matrix. Where the first assesses revenues and variable costs (both industrial and commercial), the second also includes fixed costs (again, both industrial and commercial), and the third introduces further classes of components, deriving not only from characteristic but also financial management.

---

2   Cf. Danovi and Quagli (2010).

PRODUCTS-MARKETS MATRICES

The first matrix, with variable revenues and costs, presents market segments in the columns and product lines along the rows.

Revenue figures are directly deduced from the general accounts by diversifying revenue among different product-market combinations, further simplified by sales statistics that reclassify values according to different criteria. Gross revenues, including adjustments and any returns, must then be compared with net volumes to further identify the quality of company production. The different cells of the matrix host the revenues of the various combinations: the totals for each market segment and product line are set out in appropriately structured sum cells, which converge on the general total of revenues. These summary values may be slightly different from the homologous entries in the income statement due to the omission of subdivisions deemed insignificant. An interesting peculiarity that may come to light is the correlation of certain products and markets. That is to say that each production line is specific to a market that does not receive other products.

As mentioned in the introduction, the costs in this first section include industrial and commercial variable costs. It should be noted that this configuration is particularly representative of companies with a (proportionally) lower incidence of fixed costs on total costs. This is generally due to a small number of staff and support services determining fixed costs compared to the variability of volumes, and therefore costs, produced. Moreover, since the production process is less involved, fixed costs are of less relevance to instrumental amortization.

In the table, the variable costs of different product-market configurations are assigned by market segments, not by product lines. This is because the macro-item of variable commercial costs depends on the market in which products are placed, and the levels of differentiation in commercial policies have repercussions for the range of variable unitary commercial costs in different market segments. For example, from a territorial standpoint, transport costs for sales in a commercial joint must account for the geographical distance of the market segment. The direct allocation of the various variable commercial costs to the relevant segments is also not particularly complex, although some problems may occur with indirect costs. Adjusting the previous example to a divisional model distinct from the basic geographical criterion, a correct allocation of transport costs on sales would require approximate methods based on rational imputation.

Conversely, industrial variable costs—materials, labor, services— are specific to each product line: they depend solely on production, and are not influenced by the production sector in which the goods are placed. Variations in industrial variable costs for the same product in different markets may occur when a company implements productive customizations that endow goods destined for certain markets with specific finishes. This is the case for companies that produce to order as the various unitary industrial variable costs demand a more analytical taxonomy of the product lines, such that industrial variable costs must be calculated separately for each product. Some industrial variable costs can, however, be omitted during reclassification due to their limited significance and incidence.

The matrix therefore contains the total commercial variable costs and the allocation of industrial variable costs for various product lines in each market segment. From this first scheme, it is possible to calculate the margin of commercial contribution, which indicates the capacity of each market segment to help cover industrial costs and generate a residual surplus. Applying this same reasoning to each product line, we obtain the margin of industrial contribution. This is particularly significant when applied to companies that have a reduced extension of the production cycle or a high incidence of material cost (for example, sub-supply companies or semi-finished products).

The cumulative data of the industrial contribution margins per product line and the commercial contribution margins per market segment are set out in summary. A further box contains the total contribution margin, determined by the difference between total revenues and the sum of industrial variable costs and commercial variable costs: this index expresses the company's ability to cover fixed costs and provides a basis for calculating the operating lever (also called operating contribution margin).

From the table, it is also possible to compare industrial and commercial variable costs with the quantity sold to obtain a variable unit cost, useful for planning purposes.

Especially if there are no substantial changes to production processes and expected market prices, it is possible to apply these (historicized) percentages of cost incidence on revenues to define a credible forecast of the income statement.

Products-markets matrix with variable revenues and costs[3]

		REVENUES								
		MKT 1	MKT 2	...	MKT i	...	MKT n	TOT. MKT	*IVC*	*ICM*
REVENUES	PROD. A									
	PROD. B									
	...									
	PROD. J									
	...									
	PROD. Z									
	TOT. PROD.							Tot. Rev.		
	CVC								Tot. VC	
	CCM									TCM

The second matrix assumes a more complex configuration due to the inclusion of fixed industrial and commercial costs, which are attributed to the different product lines and market segments, respectively. This matrix is necessary with the increasing quantitative relevance of company fixed costs, especially those related to manufacturing and marketing. The diagnostic set-up is based on the previously explained table, and demonstrates the flexibility of this evaluation and control system for specific business complexities.

To explain the second matrix, we must first examine the class of special industrial fixed costs. Special costs represent ceasing or differential costs, which include increased charges derived from

---

3   MKT: Market; PROD: Product; IVC: Industrial Variable Costs; CVC: Commercial Variable Costs; ICM: Industrial Contribution Margin; CCM: Commercial Contribution Margin; Rev: Revenues; VC: Variable Costs; TCM: Total Contribution Margin.

the physical technical transformation phase (such as instrumental amortization, salaries for non-operative personnel, use of third party assets, maintenance services, design and assistance), and therefore assume a central role in the elimination or outsourcing outcomes for one or more production lines. The higher charges apply exclusively to specific products or product lines. There are only choices for special fixed costs because:

- special fixed costs effect the elimination or maintenance of product lines, and the manufacture or purchase of possible products or parts of them;
- special fixed costs take on greater objectivity when evaluating the allocation of cost components;
- special fixed costs offer fewer complications for administrative-management surveys.

Special industrial fixed costs, which are specific to each product line, are also unaffected by the market segments in which they are merged. In the matrix's graphic structure, they are therefore placed in a new column next to the industrial contribution margin.

On the other hand, commercial fixed costs are considered special by market and not by product. These costs are then placed in a row immediately below the commercial contribution margin.

Subtracting the commercial fixed costs from the commercial contribution margin, we obtain the commercial operating margin. Where operating refers to the company's characteristic functions (production and marketing), this margin indicates the contribution of each market segment to covering residual costs; it finds an epilogue in a further line. The difference between this margin and net revenues indicates the impact of a company's commercial activity.

Similarly, by subtracting the industrial fixed costs from the industrial contribution margin, we obtain the industrial operating margin. This column indicates how much each product line puts towards remaining costs.

Finally, by subtracting the sum of the special industrial fixed costs and commercial fixed costs from the total contribution margin, the resulting total operating margin indicates the impact of characteristic operating functions on total revenues. This operating margin, however, does not include the net common industrial and commercial costs.

Products-markets matrix with variable and fixed revenues and costs[4]

	MKT 1	MKT 2	...	MKT i	...	MKT n	TOT. MKT	IVC	ICM	IFC	IOM
PROD. A											
PROD. B											
...											
PROD. J											
...											
PROD. Z											
TOT. PROD							Tot. Rev.				
CVC								Tot. VC			
CCM									TCM		
CFC										Tot. FC	
COM											TOM

In pre-default situations, important indications of recovery from a company in crisis include a gradual freeing of corporate financing needs and attempts to increase capital turnover and optimize the composition of sources.

Analysis and valuations of working capital management are then particularly useful, as a reduction in investment in this area leads to a reduction in financial requirements: it is evident that loans and inventories, which are critical to operating working capital, create value in a substantially indirect manner. The impact of reducing investment intensity leads to a proportionally broader program of economic efficiency.

Therefore, the income assessment for investments in working capital—commodities and trade receivables—assumes considerable importance, and the economic components expressed in the matrices must prepare the program for an economic analysis suitable for verifying financial management. In other words, it may be premature, or even misleading, to evaluate the profitability or sustainability of a business line or plan based on results obtained before financial management is

---

4   IFC: Industrial Fixed Costs; CFC: Commercial Fixed Costs; IOM: Industrial Operating Margin; COM: Commercial Operating Margin; FC: Fixed Costs; TOM: Total Operating Margin.

assessed, especially if customers with high bargaining power force the company to immobilize trade receivables due to granted extensions. This third matrix therefore involves investments in working capital that are denoted as financial charges and are therefore listed on income statements relating to product lines and market segments.

It must be said that if investment in stocks of raw materials do not correspond unequivocally to a market segment,

Product J → Market i = FALSE

it is more difficult to attribute them to individual product-market combinations after. It would be necessary to calculate or hypothesize average storage times by quantity of product according to the purchase methods of customers belonging to the different market segments: to simplify these cases, the entire investment in goods is attributed to the product line as a whole. It is also possible to proceed with weighting coefficients, which, even if approximate, offer a method of distribution appropriate to the analysis' purpose. We therefore add a column for the financial burdens of investments in stocks to the products-markets matrix, appropriately denied specificity if we have the detail—possibly existing—of raw materials dedicated to specific product lines. The financial burden, if not already provided by the stock accounts, can be calculated by interpolating the report (monthly, quarterly, etc.) of investments made and applying the average interest rate of the loans received.

We recall the predetermined range of industrial variable costs or special fixed costs of the inventory valuation. If the uncertainty is to be reduced, complex weighting calculations of the historical rates applied to individual loans will have to be made based on the size and specific duration of the loans, appropriately separated from implicit interests on commercial liabilities. It may also be necessary to identify the financial charges related to investments in loans: these considerations appear to be more immediate, and it is easy to locate the direct connections between each customer, the related credit and the product to which the accounting record refers by going through the general accounts.

For greater simplification, it is possible to include a separate row for the total credits in each market segment. Subtracting the financial charges generated by investments in inventories from the industrial operating margin, we obtain the industrial net margin.

The commercial net margin is deduced by subtracting the financial charges on receivables from the commercial operating margin.

Products-markets matrix with figurative financial charges[5]

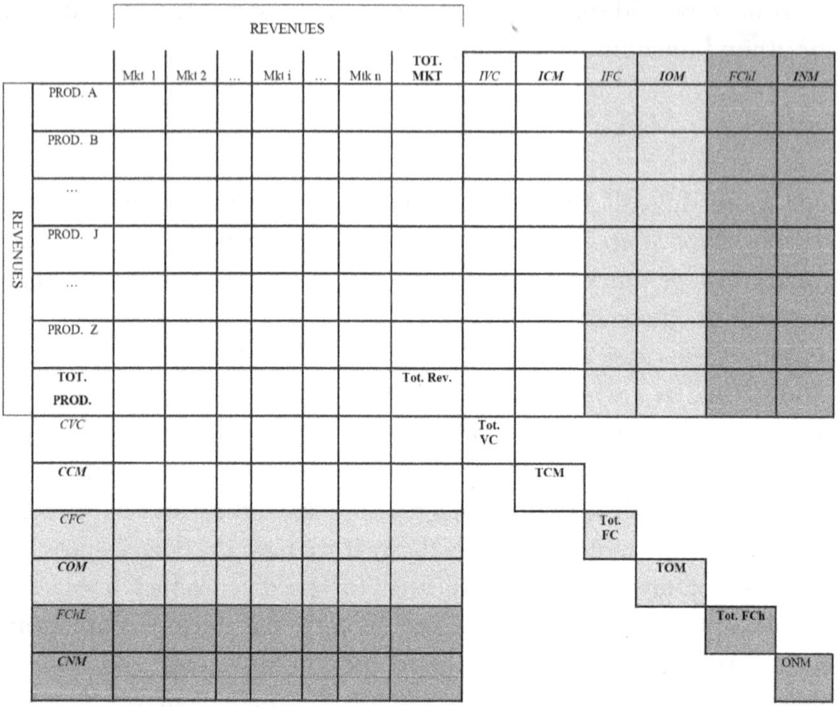
REVENUES
Mkt 1
Mkt 2
...
Mkt i
...
Mtk n
TOT. MKT
IVC
ICM
IFC
IOM
FChI
INM
REVENUES
PROD. A
PROD. B
...
PROD. J
...
PROD. Z
TOT. PROD.
Tot. Rev.
CVC
Tot. VC
CCM
TCM
CFC
Tot. FC
COM
TOM
FChL
Tot. FCh
CNM
ONM

5 FChI: Financial Charges on Inventories; FChL: Financial Charges on Loans; INM: Industrial Net Margin; CNM: Commercial Net Margin; FCh: Financial Charges; ONM: Operating Net Margin.

THE VALUATION OF BUSINESS BRANCHES WITH THE INCOME METHOD

We now examine how the income method provides support for achieving the most complete performance evaluations of each business unit. The income method belongs to the general family of flow models, which discount financial and income flows.

The theoretical contribution is convergent in the general formula:

$$W = \sum_{i=0}^{n} Fi \cdot vi$$

where:

W = the value of the corporate product-market segment under valuation, i.e. the broader business segment that includes other segments that are otherwise similar, such that further separation is inconsequential to analysis;
Fi = the flow, financial or income;
vi = the discounting factor of each flow.

Through this approach, the value of a company's economic capital is measured as the sum of all future flows, discounted at the time of valuation.

Using the margins according to segment or segment groups as derived from the matrices, we examine the use of income flows in contrast to financial ones.

The reasons for using income streams to evaluate economic capital appear throughout corporate literature. Gino Zappa (1946, p. 76) claimed that "capital is a single value, resulting from the capitalization of future income." Capital varies according to the variation of future income and the chosen income discount rate; capital therefore derives from income, and income is the true original value.

The income method is also effective because income is directly linked to the results of operations. Cash flows, on the other hand, show apparent results, which are difficult to interpret, especially where it is necessary to consider the accrual principle instead of cash basis accounting, the former considered not significant and ambiguous. Income flows express the result produced, while cash flows express the liquidity released.

Based on these considerations, the general formula is proposed below, with appropriate references to economic income flows:

$$W = Ra_{\overline{n}|i}$$

where:

W = the value of the business segment to be evaluated;
R = average prospective income, or the expected income in the coming years;
n = number of future years;
i = discount rate.

Over an infinite time horizon, economic capital would coincide with the current value of a perpetual income, with an installment represented by the prospective average income:

$$W = R/i$$

In this hypothesis, it would be necessary to:

- quantify average prospective income through the systemization of multi-year strategic programs based on previous financial statements;
- identify a congrouous time horizon;
- apply a discounting rate consistent with the current economic situation and the business risks faced.

This estimation model mainly applies to:

- the evaluation of the probability of default;
- situations where reliable forecasts on future flows can be constructed;
- companies in which assets are of little importance;

- transfers or sales of business units;
- acquisitions and joint ventures.

PROSPECTIVE AVERAGE INCOME

To determine prospective average income, we must calculate the Integrated Economic Result (IER). From the margins calculated in the previous matrices, or from partial aggregates of the same, we now normalize, and possibly integrate, other unexpressed accounting values. The recalibrated value is then adjusted for inflation.

It is also necessary to ensure that other elements useful to maintaining the significance of the IER, such as extraordinary income components and latent costs, unrelated to ordinary operations or otherwise, remain unchanged. The tax component of the tax base so normalized must then be recalculated.

The detailed calculation procedure is summarized in the following table:

ONM

NORMALIZATION OF EXTRAORDINARY COMPONENTS

+ EXTRAORDINARY CHARGES

− EXTRAORDINARY INCOME

+/− AVERAGE VALUE OF EXTRAORDINARY COMPONENTS

INSERT LATENT COSTS

− MANAGERIAL REMUNERATION

− FIGURATIVE COSTS OF RENTING

− COMPUTED INTERESTS

OTHER CORRECTIVES FOR NORMALIZATION

+/− NORMALIZATION OF INCOME COMPONENTS OUT OF
     MANAGEMENT
+/− LEASING FEES

...

NGI - **NORMALIZED GROSS INCOME**

TAX CORRECTIVES

NNI - **NORMALIZED NET INCOME**

Extraordinary income components are made up of extraordinary gains and losses (for example, deriving from the sale of non-instrumental goods), extraordinary non-existences (for example, penalties from tax disputes, divestiture of assets caused by third parties or claims) and extraordinary contingencies (for example, insurance reimbursements).

Normalization does not eliminate these values, but substitutes them with more accurate averages based on historical series. In this way, the effects of multiple exercises are homogenized, avoiding excitations or depressions caused by abnormal manifestations of the reported values.

For example, if a company has extraordinary components in the four years preceding the year n for which we intend to normalize income, such that:

$$n - 4 = a; n - 3 = b; n - 2 = c; n - 1 = d; n = e$$

We then calculate the arithmetic average $AV = (a + b + c + d + e) / 5$. From there, we subtract the extraordinary element e from the ONM of year n, and add AV.

For latent costs associated with a business and its production plant, we analyze:

- the lower value of the remuneration received by the entrepreneur and/or those with authority over average standard payments;
- any figurative rents of buildings used in ordinary management, i.e. the hypothetical revenues achieved by these properties if they were rented;
- the computed interest on the invested capital, considered non-verified returns on capital as it is not used in financial investments otherwise.

Although there may be other categories of values, those listed are considered the most significant for evaluating company performance. The previous value calculated removes non-management components that are not directly relevant to the typical activity from income, after which the result is normalized by substituting average values that represent the flow of income under normal market conditions.

Leasing contracts accounted for using the equity method are a special case (albeit increasingly infrequent due to the adoption of

IAS 17): this method notes leasing fees as a single value in the income statement; in the balance sheet, they are included in memorandum accounts. Income normalization should then be considered through the financial method, which lists the value of the leased asset under assets and liabilities in the payable as a payable to the leasing company; the income statement calculates the depreciation on the value of the asset and the financial component of the fees.

The normalization process must also be adjusted to balance the cost of the leasing fee and the amortization that would be calculated on the leased asset. The successive elements of financial statements, i.e. write-downs, provisions and future charges, must then be verified. Finally, the tax burden must be corrected by accurately estimating the actual commitment for the year, including net deferred tax assets and/ or deferred taxes.

For the income method, it is also necessary to choose between a finite or infinite time horizon approach. Corporate literature and professional practice prefer perpetual annuity algorithms, and therefore unlimited time. This propensity is based on the business continuity principle, which views a company as an institution destined to last over time. From a mathematical point of view, it is also evident that the two formulas will gradually converge as the number of years n increases, with significant impact for $n \geq 30$ if the interest rate applied is close to the average Effective Global Rate when $n = 0$.

Nonetheless, it may be necessary to use a fixed time, albeit not less than five years, for greater alignment with specific product and project cycles, both in agreed circumstances, and technological progressions.

Once the corrective measures are drawn up, the discount rate must be determined. This is the most complex element to define because of its functions:

- to discount the presumed future financial flows: the higher the discount rate, the lower the current value of these flows. From a pragmatic standpoint, the rate should therefore be increased as the future of expected income flows becomes increasingly uncertain, due, in part, to the removal of estimate times;
- to express business risk, i.e. to have a margin of confidence for the possibility that the alleged discounted income flows will not be achieved: a higher risk sensitivity will increase the rate chosen;
- to summarize the market trends in which a company or the single

product-market segment under evaluation operates, based on profitability indices in the product sector;

- to adjust the nominal aspect for inflationary trends, through spread corrections on marked price increases or decreases.

According to conventional doctrine, there are two main methodologies for identifying the discount rate: the criterion of the opportunity rate (or equivalent rate) and the criterion of the cost of capital. The first summarizes the yield in alternate investments with the same level of risk; it is therefore very important to standardize risk levels. The second identifies a discounting rate that represents the cost of capital.

For more predictive deterministic evaluations, we will proceed with the criterion of the opportunity rate.

Literature agrees on these three fundamental components of the opportunity rate:

$$i = i^* + r + l$$

where:

i = discount rate of prospective average income, possibly declined on the individual product-market segment;

i^* = return rate of alternate investments with no risk. It also represents the Internal Rate of Return (IRR) of a loan whose correct recasting is essentially guaranteed, for example, the rate of return on government bonds within 12 months or the medium-long term, depending on the timeframe considered in the valuation;

r = the company's risk of not reaching presumed future income: this is the most difficult component to determine, as it is related to various management variables such as the contraction of commercial relationships (customers and suppliers), immediate insolvency, unfavorable legislative changes, negative economic situation and a generalized sector crisis. The appraisal must therefore consider a constant of carefully argued risk to valorize the related *vulnera*;

l = lower liquidity of investment in the company's capital compared to alternate investments. In other words, as certain investments, especially public bonds whose return is accounted for in the first component, liquidate almost immediately compared to the capital invested in the company, the discount rate must be increased to anticipate the time required for capital to liquidate.

PRESENT VALUE AND EXTENDED PRESENT VALUE

From the product-market matrices, we calculated both aggregate and unitary annual margins, from which we further derived the income flows vector. We will now analyze the equivalent rate. This rate is suitable for comparing the remuneration of current operations with that of any disposable strategies or post-reorganization business scenarios, to understand the extent of default risk and possible escape routes to mitigate the loss given default.

In practice, we calculate the Net Present Value (NPV), at the equivalent rate, by dividing the sum of the elements of the flows vector by $(1 + i)$ to increase time:

$$NPV = \sum_{s=0}^{n} NNI_s \cdot (1 + i)^{-s}$$

In the case that the same positive *NPV* is produced, it is necessary to choose the allocation that ensures higher values.

Here, we introduce the concept of Strategic Business Areas (SBA), wherein a competitive strategy is adopted when specific biunivocal relations (also identified or selected as performing) between individual segment-market partitions in the tables are present.

In order to protect risk positions, a company's organizational model is redefined to focus on the divisional system and to alienate non-strategic business areas, so that a more functional management system is in place for the renewed business period.

A company's reorganization is therefore oriented around valorizing resources and assets and recovering economic conditions, thus creating greater value than the current value generated by a company heading towards crisis. This is implemented through:

- increasing normalized income flows;
- improving the discounting rate through the general reduction of risks;
- reducing debt and total invested capital.

We have compiled the most effective criterion in the Extended Present Value method to improve the quality of the recovery strategy[6]:

$$VR = \sum SBA + Po + Op + Iacc$$

where:

VR = the value of the restored company;
ΣSBA = the sum of the value of the company's strategic business areas;
Po = the value of the strategic portfolio (any greater—or less, if negative—value of synergies between the SBAs);
Op = the value of the real options made possible by reorganization;
$Iacc$ = the value of accessory investments.

This method requires a thorough quantitative and qualitative knowledge of the company and of the general business, as well as of each product-market segment and SBA. Implementation involves quantitatively and qualitatively determining the flows, identifying the most suitable time horizon and defining the risks, expressed and latent, using appropriate equivalent rates. From this related analysis, it will be possible to determine the most suitable out-of-court solutions between: recovery strategy, rent or sale, and settlement (this being the last option as it leads inexorably to the termination of the SBA or of the company as a whole).

Provided that the current value is maintained, and factoring in the assumed value of the company in liquidation (VL) or cession (VC), consolidation will proceed if it is shown that:

$$VR > VC \wedge VR > VL$$

With these considerations, the evaluator will understand the company's profitability and sustainability according to financial commitments undertaken. By calculating and monitoring future income streams, he will be able to interpret the possible discontinuity or criticality of individual product-market segments and implement pre-default recovery strategies to protect against insolvencies[7].

---

6   Cf. Yun (2011).
7   Cf. Migliori (2013).

2. NON-DETERMINISTIC APPROACHES TO BUSINESS AND FINANCIAL EVALUATIONS. MARKOV MODEL

SOME APPLICATIONS OF STOCHASTIC MODELS

Linking Synthesis

R ecently, there has been particular interest in applying mathematical models to interpretations and simulations of financial markets. In all respects, they represent complex, non-linear, open systems characterized by chaotic dynamics. Similar conditions apply to individual mathematical-financial problems. A purely deterministic approach, such as that widely used to measure current value, even in a scheme of compound interest:

$$C = M(1 + i)^{-t}$$

returns a rough and static representation of reality that is insensitive to other variables of decay when time is considered *periodal*. Similar findings are noted in exercises carried out in assumed conditions of certainty, such as the calculation of the NPV and/or the IRR when deciding on a financial transaction (or comparative between several options), using only reference numeric values.

By evolving calculations of present value for a continuous annuity such that time is fractional in m periods of infinitesimal duration, m then tends towards infinity. The representation of payments over time is therefore a continuous and uniform flow:

$$\overline{a}_{\overline{n}|i} = \lim_{m \to \infty} a_{\overline{n}|i}^{(m)} = \frac{i}{\delta} \, a_{\overline{n}|i}$$

where $\delta = \ln(1 + i)$ is the instantaneous intensity of interest.

An important contribution is provided by the pricing and evaluation models that characterize studies of complex financial products from the last 70 years. The paradigm shifts to consider the randomness and peculiar uncertainty of certain variables of financial phenomena (at least in some cases), in addition to their deterministic nature. A fundamental result is found through probabilistic calculations that determine probability spaces (Ω, F, Pr). In this triad, Ω identifies the space of events, F is the σ-algebra of Ω—the set of properties and/or information located within an elected partition—and Pr is a probability. Where (Ω, F) is a measurable space, if (1) $Pr(\varnothing) = 0$ e $Pr(\Omega) = 1$ and (2) for each succession $\{E_n\}_n \in F$ mutually disjointed ($i \neq j \Rightarrow Fi \cap Fj = \varnothing$), Pr will be:

$$\Pr\left(\bigcup_{i=1}^{\infty} E_i\right) = \sum_{i=1}^{\infty} \Pr(E_i)$$

Furthermore, a relevant expression of the matter is the establishment of the random variable (X), especially when treated as a continuous variable which, for each real x, is known if the function of breakdown $F(x)$ or the function of probability density $f(x)$ is known, such that:

$$F(x) = \Pr(-\infty < X < x) = \Pr(X < x) = \int_{-\infty}^{x} f(\omega)d\omega$$

where $f(x) = \frac{dF(x)}{dx}$ produces interesting distributions (e.g. normal or Gaussian bell charts), which have wide applications for modelling scientific phenomena.

This sequence of mathematical-financial calculations carefully assesses the uncertainty and randomness inherent in dynamic and complex systems—such as markets and expected returns on investment—and produces a more accurate prediction that is crucial for determining portfolio strategies.

If a differential equation with a single variable function operating as its order, $y^{(n)} = (x, y, ..., y^{(n-1)})$, produces an integral with a unique evolution, the stochastic process can be used to represent the evolution of a family of random variables, or a complex system, over time.

Some trends or motions appear to be completely unpredictable: Brownian motion, named after Scottish botanist Robert Brown, or 'random walk' are related to such random and continuous trends.

French statistician and mathematician, Louis Bachelier (1900, p. 47), observed that stock prices followed this type of motion.

Mathematically, it is defined by $(B(t), t \geq 0)$ and is characterized by independent, stationary and Gaussian increments.

The complexity of reality makes it difficult to identify all variables and random relationships between events. Stochastic models therefore add a random element σdX to deterministic equations, where $(S(t), t \geq 0)$:

$$\frac{dS}{S} = \mu dt + \sigma dX$$

The σdX element factors in the shock caused by potential exogenous factors or unknown information (e.g. volatility is a Gaussian shock with $\sigma > 0$).

The deterministic $\frac{ds}{s} = \mu dt$ can easily be written as $d \log S = \mu dt$, in which we observe exponential growth (for example, μ—drift coefficient—is the average price of a good). However, writing $d \log S = \mu dt + \sigma dX$, and integrating between 0 and t, leads to the erroneous solution:

$$\log \frac{S(t)}{S(0)} = \mu t + \sigma(X(t) - X(0)) = \mu t + \sigma X(t)$$

This last writing is incorrect, as the diffusion term, σdX, forcibly extends integration to consider the stochastic differential present in the function (Lemma di Itō[8]).

---

8   The lemma is in fact an extension on a stochastic function of Taylor series development, the latter applicable only for deterministic functions. In this case, dX is not an exact differential, but the random component of a random variable. Let $x(t)$ be an Itō process that thus satisfies the stochastic differential equation: $dx(t) = a(x,t)dt + b(x,t)dX_t$. Also, let f be a function

Issues relating to credit and financial risk assessment

Especially for insolvency forecasting, business evaluation models by banks and other institutions are limited by univariate procedures. A financial economic assessment for credit analysis is essentially based on budget indicators.

The examination is carried out according to single factors, after which results are organized and compared in a coherent system involving sector data, historical series and qualitiative factors.

Although not all indicators show a significant diagnostic capacity, these models have produced good results for individual companies. Some research (e.g. Beaver, 2010) has shown their discrete predictive capabilities, especially with the use of the cash flow ratio on total debts that, properly weighted, correctly classified up to 80% of companies assessed based on the Probability of Default (PD)—almost 90% at t − 1, where t is the default year.

However, the lack of synthesis between the various elements assessed, such as profitability, financial structure and available liquidity, together with a Bayesian basic facility, means these applications are hardly conducive to more complex assessments, on longer period or portfolio.

This sequential investigation should be replaced by a mathematical method that simultaneously considers all variables involved.

For this reason, in addition to accounting for the cost of provisions, variables for risk segments, and the potential necessity of enabling appropriate mechanisms of mitigation or immunization for losses and sufferings, the new challenge is in providing the system with more predictive instruments. We need systems capable of capturing the results of forbearance procedures or stochastically evaluating the impact of a new investment (including financial) on a company's settlement, development and outlook rating.

---

having continuous second derivative: then $f(x(t),t)$ is still a process of Itō, from which $df(x(t),t) = \left(a(x,t)\frac{\partial f}{\partial x} + \frac{\partial f}{\partial t} + \frac{1}{2}\left(b(x,t)\right)^2\frac{\partial^2 f}{\partial x^2}\right)dt + b(x,t)\frac{\partial f}{\partial x}dX_t.$ The integral of Itō, obtainable from the lemma, broadens and generalizes the Riemann integral for stochastic functions. It does not have a geometrical meaning; it is not an area.

The linear discriminating analysis proposed by Fisher (1936) offers a step forward, with a multivariate perspective that generates a score of classification:

$$S_j = a_1 X_{1j} + a_2 X_{2j} + \ldots + a_i X_{ij} + \ldots + a_n X_{nj}$$

where:

S_j = the score of the j-th enterprise;
X_{ij} = the descriptive variable of the i-th feature of the j-th enterprise (x_i = column vector of those variables);
a_j = the coefficient of variable X_{ij}.

On two (or more) known populations A and B (i.e. "Non-performing" and "in Bonis" within the time t), company j may be assigned to A or B, depending on the distance of S_j from the average scores of the two populations:

$$S_j = (\overline{x}_A - \overline{x}_B) V^{-1} x_j$$

where $\overline{x}_A$ and $\overline{x}_B$ are the column vectors of the averages of the variables of the two samples extracted from populations A and B, and V is the n by n matrix of the variances and covariances that is calculated on the union of the two samples compared to the average $\overline{x}$. If the populations are multinormal, the classification criterion leads to a quadratic discriminating function.

A simplified extension of the model (in which the populations are set in the same matrix of variance and covariance) comes from the Altman Z-score (1993, p. 202) and its empirical research: this model showed an accuracy of 95% one year prior to the unfavorable event or default (Error α = 6%; β = 3%).

Particular emphasis is also put on the recent guidelines of the European Banking Authority (EBA), especially in relation to the renewed flows of some international accounting standards, including IFRS 9 which introduced the concept of expected credit losses. The EBA has dictated specific technical provisions to verify the presence of conditions of probable default.

MARKOV CHAINS

One-step Markov process

In a family of random variables $X = \{X_t : t \in T\}$, if set T is discrete, the stochastic process is a discrete-time process with the notation $\{X_n : n \in N\}$. However, if set T is continuous, it is called a continuous-time process because it coincides with R or R^+ or represents any subset of R. Depending on the number of values assumed by causal variables, when countable, we define processes as discrete in discrete time and as steps in continuous time.

Let us focus on a discrete-time process for this last hypothesis.

In a process $\{X_n\}$, $n = 1, 2, \ldots$, where each X_n variable can only assume finite or infinite countable values—not necessarily the same for each X_n, all values that the set of X_n variables can have are defined by the space of the states S, either as infinite set $S^\infty = \{0, 1, 2, \ldots\}$ or finished set $S^d = \{0, 1, 2, \ldots, d\}$.

If $X_n = i$ means that the process at the instant n is in the state i, then we calculate probability as:

$$P_{ij}^n = P(X_{n+1} = j | X_n = i)$$

Where this process will be in the state j at the next $n + 1$ instant, we define the Markov chain in the reported process $\{X_n\}$, $n = 1, 2, \ldots$, as:

$$P(X_{n+1} = j | X_{n-1} = i, X_{n-1} = i_{n-1}, \ldots, X_0 = i_0)$$
$$= P(X_{n+1} = j | X_n = i) = P_{ij}^n$$

Every time the probabilities are significant for each state $i_0, i_1, \ldots, i_{n-1}, i, j$ and for each $n \geq 0$, P_{ij}^n probabilities represent a one-step transition probability of a Markov chain.

This means that for every instant n, assuming the present state of the process is X_n, and its past $X_{n-1}, \ldots, X_1, X_0$, the law that determines the future state X_{n+1} depends only on the present and is independent from the past. The P_{ij}^n represent the probabilities of transition from state i to state j, dependent only on the instant n.

A Markov chain, for which:

$$P(X_{n+1} = j | X_n = i) = P_{ij}$$

And, therefore:

$$P_{ij} = P(X_1 = j | X_0 = i)$$

where it is called a homogeneous Markov chain when $n \geq 0$. According to this law, however, the probability of transition from state i to state j in a step, does not depend on either that instant or where that transition takes place.

We represent below the conditions satisfied by the properties of this conditional probability:

$$P_{ij} \geq 0; \quad i, j \geq 0; \quad \sum_{j \in S} P_{ij} = 1$$

The matrix P is derived from the probability of transition to a step, and is specific to this type of Markov chain:

$$P^\infty = \begin{bmatrix} P_{00} & P_{01} & P_{02} & \cdots & P_{0j} & \cdots \\ P_{10} & P_{11} & P_{12} & \cdots & P_{1j} & \cdots \\ P_{20} & P_{21} & P_{22} & \cdots & P_{2j} & \cdots \\ \vdots & \vdots & \vdots & \ddots & \vdots & \vdots \\ P_{i0} & P_{i1} & P_{i2} & \cdots & P_{ij} & \cdots \\ \vdots & \vdots & \vdots & \ddots & \vdots & \vdots \end{bmatrix}$$

The matrix P, or the 'one-step transition matrix,' determines the evolution of the homogeneous Markov chain for every instant where $n \geq 1$. Each element of the matrix is greater than or equal to 0, and the sum of the elements in each row is equal to 1. It is therefore a stochastic matrix.

In the event that the space of the states is finished, the matrix P takes the form $d \times d$:

$$P^d = \begin{bmatrix} P_{11} & P_{12} & P_{13} & \cdots & P_{1d} \\ P_{10} & P_{11} & P_{12} & \cdots & P_{2d} \\ P_{20} & P_{21} & P_{22} & \cdots & P_{3d} \\ \vdots & \vdots & \vdots & \ddots & \vdots \\ P_{d1} & P_{d2} & P_{d3} & \cdots & P_{dd} \end{bmatrix}$$

An application

We can apply this model to the player's downfall theorem, developed below. Imagine an entrepreneur makes a series of investments, characterized by a given level of risk, and full remuneration of capital invested, in the positive case. For each investment, he has a probability $p = a$ to win and a probability $q = 1 - p = b$ (b > a) to lose the invested capital. We assume that the entrepreneur will stop investing when his wealth has reached value N, or when he has lost everything and his equity is equal to 0.

X_n is the amount of the entrepreneur's fortune after n investments. The family of values prior to X_n is a Markov chain. In fact, if $X_n = i$ (for $0 < i < N$), then for every possible situation at previous instants:

$$P(X_{n+1} = i + 1 | X_n = i, X_{n-1} = i_{n-1}, X_{n-2} = i_{n-2}, \ldots, X_1 = i_1, X_0 = i_0)$$
$$= a$$

The fortune of the entrepreneur at instant $n + 1$ depends only on his fortune at the previous instant. The transition probabilities are $P_{i,i+1} = a$; $P_{i,i-1} = b$ for $0 < i < N$; $P_{0,0} = 1$; $P_{N,N} = 1$:

$$P = \begin{bmatrix} 1 & 0 & 0 & 0 & 0 & 0 \\ b & 0 & a & 0 & 0 & 0 \\ 0 & b & 0 & a & 0 & 0 \\ 0 & 0 & b & 0 & a & 0 \\ 0 & 0 & 0 & b & 0 & a \\ 0 & 0 & 0 & 0 & 0 & 1 \end{bmatrix}$$

In a one-step transition matrix for N = 5, the space of states consists of 5 + 1 elements. The elements $P_{0,0} = 1$ e $P_{N,N} = 1$ show that at the instant $n^* \geq 0$, the chain leads to state 0 or state N. These states are temporary, however, because $P(X_{n+1} = 0|X_n = 0) = 1$ and $P(X_{n+1} = N|X_n = N) = 1$ for every $n \geq n^*$.

Multi-step transition probabilities

$\{X_n\}$ is a Markov chain with the space of states S. For every $n \geq 1$, $P_{ij}^{(n)}$ is the probability that the chain has transitioned from state i to state j, n instants before:

$$P_{ij}^{(n)} = P(X_{n+m} = j|X_m = i)$$

As the chain is homogeneous, $P_{ij}^{(n)}$ does not depend on m:

$$P_{ij}^{(n)} = P(X_n = j|X_0 = i)$$

and $P_{ij}^{(1)} = P_{ij}$:

$$P_{ij}^{(n)} = \sum_{h \in S} P_{ih}^{n-1} P_{hj}$$

therefore:

$$P_{ij}^{(n)} = \frac{P(X_n = j, X_0 = i)}{P(X_0 = i)} = \sum_{h \in S} \frac{P(X_n = j, X_{n-1} = h, X_0 = i)}{P(X_0 = i)}$$

$$= \sum_{h \in S} P(X_n = j|X_{n-1} = h, X_0 = i)P(X_{n-1} = h|X_0 = i)$$

$$= \sum_{h \in S} P(X_n = j|X_{n-1} = h)P_{ih}^{n-1} = \sum_{h \in S} P(X_1 = j|X_0 = h)P_{ih}^{n-1}$$

from which we return to:

$$P_{ij}^{(n)} = \sum_{h \in S} P_{ih}^{n-1} P_{hj}$$

This formula is a special type of Chapman-Kolmogorov equation, and calculates the probability of transition in n-steps. We can build the $P^{(n)}$ matrix, whose elements are the probabilities $P_{ij}^{(n)}$, such that $P^{(n)} = P^{(n-1)}$. P is then the product of matrices, for infinite values. From this observation, we deduce $P^{(2)} = P \cdot P = P^2$ and $P^{(n)} = P^n$. Also, $P^{(m+n)} = P^{(m)} \cdot P^{(n)}$, from:

$$P_{ij}^{(m+n)} = \sum_{h \in S} P_{ih}^{(m)} P_{hj}^{(n)}$$

Particular importance is given to the probability π^n, which assumes that the chain is in a certain state i at the instant n:

$$\pi_k^n = P(X_n = k), \nabla k \in S$$

Two-state Markov chain

Recall the considerations made in the preamble to this chapter about the increasing need to assess company rating and deduce solvency perspectives.

A two-state Markov chain is a good model for such an assessment. As stated in the premise, an enterprise can be found in two states, Non-performing and in Bonis. The Non-performing state is indicated with 0 and the in Bonis state with 1. Suppose that a company is in state 0 on day n: α is the probability that it will be in state 1 on day $n + 1$, no matter where it was in the days before n. Suppose also that this same company is in state 1 on day n: β is the probability that it will be in state 0 on day $n + 1$, also regardless of its state in the days before n. The chain $\{X_n\}$ follows the evolution of a company's state during the days $n = 1, 2, ..., n$. Let us assume that neither α nor β are at the same time 0, to avoid a static system (0 or 1). Let us also assume that neither α nor β are at the same time 1, in which case the system would be deterministic at every instant from 0 to 1 (therefore $0 < \alpha + \beta < 2$). This framework then produces a Markov chain with the transition matrix:

$$P = \begin{bmatrix} 1 - \alpha & \alpha \\ \beta & 1 - \beta \end{bmatrix}$$

Resolving the recurrent equations, the n-step transition matrix is given by:

$$P^{(n)} = \frac{(1 - \alpha - \beta)^n}{\alpha + \beta} \begin{bmatrix} \alpha & -\alpha \\ -\beta & \beta \end{bmatrix} + \frac{1}{\alpha + \beta} \begin{bmatrix} \beta & \alpha \\ \beta & \alpha \end{bmatrix}$$

We then calculate the distribution of the variables X_n to determine the probability that the company is in state 0 or state 1 at the instant n:

$$P(X_n = 0) = \frac{\beta}{\alpha + \beta} + (1 - \alpha - \beta)^n (\pi_0^0 - \frac{\beta}{\alpha + \beta})$$

and:

$$P(X_n = 1) = \frac{\beta}{\alpha + \beta} + (1 - \alpha - \beta)^n (\pi_1^0 - \frac{\alpha}{\alpha + \beta})$$

Since the chain has only two states, when $n = 0$, π_0^0 represents the probability that the chain is in state 0 [$\pi_0^0 = P(X_0 = 0)$], while π_1^0 represents the probability that the chain is in state 1 [$\pi_1^0 = 1 - \pi_0^0 = P(X_0 = 1)$].

For the hypothesis $| 1 - \alpha - \beta | < 1$:

$$\lim_{n \to +\infty} P(X_n = 0) = \frac{\beta}{\alpha + \beta}$$

and:

$$\lim_{n \to +\infty} P(X_n = 0) = \frac{\alpha}{\alpha + \beta}$$

3. MACROECONOMIC THEORY OF CREDIT: A QUANTIC VIEW ON MICROFINANCE

THE SCIENCE OF QUANTUM ECONOMICS[9]

Introduction and scientific background

Across current dominant theories regarding or involving measures of economic value, money is propagated as a dimensional unit with its own distinct value and form. It is because of this very reasoning, however, that conventional economic studies and theories are destined to fail.

Take, for example, David Ricardo's (1817/1915, p. 361) analysis of the volatile value of goods: "The only qualities necessary to make a measure of value a perfect one are, that it should itself have value, and that value should be itself invariable." His research focuses on a unit of measurement that is wholly dimensional. Where current economic practice exchanges money for real goods, Ricardo parallels this transaction with a kind of barter trade, such that money becomes a physical commodity with a value equivalent to that of the goods purchased. As products and markets are heterogenous in nature, however, treating money as a physical and "invariable" value that measures value is fallible.

Quantum macroeconomic theory, by contrast, proposes that money is a numerical concept that represents the production of physical output. First theorized by Bernard Schmitt, quantum economics is grounded in the principles of two earlier economic theorists.

We begin with Adam Smith's "great wheel of circulation" (1776/1976, p. 74), which argues that money is distinct from its physical form, and therefore not a commodity: "The great wheel of

---

9   This contribution proceeds from the research work of Schmitt, Cencini and Rossi (see the references for details).

circulation is altogether different from the goods which are circulated by means of it. The revenue of the society consists altogether in those goods, and not in the wheel which circulates them." For Smith, money indicates the social value ascribed to goods produced, rather than a physical object equal in value to real output. This view is supported by Léon Walras's (1952, p. 153) idea of money as a purely numerical and non-dimensional object. Introduced in the 1930s, and pivotal to the development of quantum economic theory, is John Maynard Keynes' "monetary theory of production" (1973a, pp. 408-411), which offers a revised banking system that records money under two simultaneous transactions, as both a debit and a credit. Expanding on this observation, Keynes shifted the purview of macro demand and supply, and savings and investment as equilibrium conditions to one of logical identities. The payment of wages was also his ideal measure of economic value due to the dual nature of money, also supported by Smith's interpretation of money as the social value of goods produced:

> The prevalence of the idea that savings and investment, taken in their straightforward sense, can differ from one another, is to be explained, I think, by an optical illusion due to regarding an individual depositor's relation to his bank as being a one-sided transaction, instead of seeing it as the two-sided transaction which it actually is. (1973b, p. 81)

Further theories attributed to the advancement of quantum economics include unorthodox interpretations of Say's Law that follow on Keynes' belief that global demand and supply are logical identities; Böhm-Bawerk's theory of capital[10] in relation to time; and Knut Wicksell's (1903) view that money creation is inherent to banks.

---

10   Capital is not regarded as a factor of production alongside land and labor, but it is associated with them. Besides, its value is not measured based on the labor and land used in past production, but on its ability to produce goods in the future.

Schmitt's theory of money emissions

The theory of money emissions is an abstract framework founded on a modern conception of money that emphasizes its cyclical nature and identifies it as the factor that allows the circulation of goods.

Over two centuries ago, Adam Smith (1776/1976) realized that "the great wheel of circulation is altogether different from the goods which are circulated"—it is the totality of goods introduced to the social system, not the driving force that allows the goods to move. Schmitt (1984) recognized that the only way to understand the essence of money as a means of circulation is to view it as a momentary occurrence, rather than a reserve of wealth as it is generally perceived in its inactive phase between payments.

Schmitt therefore sees money as an instantaneous flow that does not outlast the moment of payment in a transaction between two agents in a capitalist economy[11]. Money enters the real world and is used according to the logical rules that govern modern banking. Its vehicular nature and intrinsic character provide an objective numerical measure for economic transactions. In an instantaneous cycle, money returns to its starting point the instant it is emitted, since every payment brings the creation and destruction of the immaterial substance necessary for the circulation of goods between economic agents. This innovative concept logically explains the purchasing power of money in relation to the production process. From the moment that money income results from monetizing the total costs of production, real production begins.

The theory of money emissions distinguishes the theoretical concept of money as a means of payment from its formal manifestation as momentary purchasing power. As previously stated, bank deposits do not cease to exist in the period between one payment and another. In these times, it is more appropriate to speak of bank balances rather than money.

By definition, money and payments are the same, as no money exists before or after a given payment. Though bank deposits exist in

---

11   Cf. Cencini (2001), revisited by Rossi (2006) and by Pilkington (2010).

time, it takes only an instant to insert this payment into a computerized system of bank accounts.

In this era of dematerialized money, banks are the only institutions that have the right to issue legally recognized payments through the double-entry accounting standard. The bookkeeping entries in bank ledgers in fact highlight the validity of Smith's "great wheel of circulation," and represent the real circulation of goods and services within an economy.

In order to understand the nature of bank money, it is necessary to understand its dependence on accounting procedures. While double-entry bookkeeping involves registering payments, the resulting balances (both positive and negative) are only the result of payments, not money itself. Thus double-entry bookkeeping registers the result of monetary flow but not the flow itself. The simultaneous occurrence of the manifestation of money and the execution of payments is a fundamental law of bank money that is independent of the idiosyncratic characteristics of agentic behavior.

By analyzing the accounting logic of payments and production, quantum economists also redefine Say's Law to demonstrate that global supply and demand are inevitably identical at all times.

The quantum concept of production

The theory of money emissions goes beyond the continuous time in which production takes place. The theory introduces the idea that a product can be defined by a quantum of time, in other words, an interval of continuous time emitted as an indivisible unit.

The product is the physical result of a process that takes place in continuous time; it becomes a concrete economic event when production is quantified in the form of wages. This view of economic creation parallels the theory of wave-particle duality. The instantaneous existence of economic production in the final stage of the process defines the entire period. This concept is grounded in Schmitt's (1984) logical and fascinating conclusion: "on a quantum of time, production does not take place in time but it actually is time" (p. 54). Cencini (1985) also maintains that quanta of time are a logical necessity for economic theory. Production is redefined by transforming an interval of time into a quantum, such that production defines a quantum as a real and instant emission, which "quantizes" time[12]. In extreme synthesis, according to quantum macroeconomic analysis, physical output, including the time required to physically produce it, is emitted the instant that economic production takes place. This philosophical idea of time underpins two fundamental principles of quantum economics: wages paid in exchange for production are an economic unit of measurement, and production and consumption are instantaneous events.

This concept fits perfectly into Keynes' monetary theory of production (1933/1973a), in which production is a primary economic activity that inevitably precedes any exchange. Once production is conceived as a quantum of time, money reveals its true numerical form and acts as a homogenous measure for all goods and services produced.

Money gains a positive value and therefore positive purchasing power in economic production through the conceptual association described above.

Elements of theoretical explanations

The widely accepted view of money is that it expresses a positive value—which represents purchasing power—because it is emitted by the banking system to allow economic agents to make payments. In other words, basic accounting processes give the banking system the ability of *creatio ex nihilo* for units of purchasing power. This means that a national payment system would operate in order to provide the economy with a net worth, regardless of relative production.

This notion is clearly unfounded.

In fact, double-entry bookkeeping demands the logical equivalence of both sides of the balance sheet.

Literature often posits gold as a standard monetary unit emitted in and by a country. However, this argument is incomplete, since it disregards the fact that total national production has replaced gold as an asset on the modern banking balance sheet, and that national currency is created as a liability, and is the contra account to gross

---

12　　　Cf. Schmitt (1984).

domestic product (GDP).

Similar ideas deriving from the imperfect analysis of bank money are invalidated by the lack of distinction between the form and content of payments.

It is therefore necessary to develop a bank money analysis that coincides with Smith's "great wheel of circulation." The great wheel of circulation, as Smith stated, is entirely different from the goods it circulates. Income consists wholly of the goods, and not of the wheel which allows their movement. If money were simply the counterpart of domestic product, it would be sufficient to proportionate money supply to GDP to determine the total quantitative wealth of a nation. This would, however, require viewing monetary tools as intermediary goods with a net worth to facilitate exchange between economic agents in terms of real products.

Every day we observe transactions in which money is exchanged for various goods and services. This leads to the traditional view that money does not have a crucial economic role because the exchange of goods could equally take place in the form of barter or in relation to specific goods.

Advanced monetary economics could never confirm such conclusions. A close examination of monetary transactions cannot affirm that money and goods occur simultaneously, or that they are of the same measurement (i.e. they do not possess equal nominal and real value). In reality, money is not a medium of exchange, as indicated by the neoclassical marginalist models of the general equilibrium theory[13], but a vehicle through which goods move between economic operators.

Money is the numerical form for units of purchasing power, and that was most likely understood by both Marx (1939/1973) and Keynes (1930). The key to understanding the nature of the goods being exchanged between any given agents is offered by modern monetary theory where every monetary payment is also an exchange. Furthermore, the banking system has a crucial and immutable role in issuing the numerical means for the circulation of products. Whenever a payment is made, a circular flow of money is created. As monetary intermediaries, banks both provide and recall this numerical tool from the economy.

The emission of money is at the same time the creation and the

---

13   Cf. Clower (1977) and Starr (1989).

destruction of the numerical means needed to measure the value of and circulate goods. This is substantiated by the typical workings of double-entry bookkeeping, which guarantees the instant matching of numbers entered in the assets with those present in the liabilities of any balance sheet.

The balance that agent B receives on loan from the banking system to buy goods from counterpart A is compensated in the accounts in numerical form. This represents A's right to a bank deposit of the exact same value as the price of the goods that A sells to B. Every payment has two aspects, numerical and real, and involves three entities: the payer, the payee and the banking system. In a single action, money is issued, agent B, who has access to the loan, owes a debt to the bank, while counterpart A, who receives the payment, becomes a creditor of the same bank.

The bank—or the banking system as a whole—owes A an amount equivalent to the purchasing power of the loan given to B[14].

The total domestic product (before final consumption), therefore, is the content of bank deposits, which can also identify the good *par excellence*. At the same time, bank deposits are a numerical expression of the total gross product. Before proceeding with the analysis, it is necessary to reach a formal agreement between these mutually exclusive assertions:

1. if money is indeed a good, although *sui generis*, it cannot measure real production, as money itself would need to be measured;
2. vice versa, if money is not part of a group of products, it cannot be the counterpart in any exchange in the goods market or the factors of production market.

Similarly, the microfoundations of general equilibrium models cannot truly explain the existence of a principal macroeconomic measurement of capitalist economic systems: national income.

The above-mentioned reasoning of general equilibrium models, in effect, cannot justify the emergence of a net income for the economic system. Since neoclassical economic theory maintains that income is generated from the difference between sales and purchases in a goods market, it is necessary to overcome this dialectic gap:

---

14   Cf. Graziani (1989) and Rossi (1998).

On a more sophisticated level, the logical flaw of received monetary theory can be best highlighted by referring to the conception of absolute exchange worked out by B. Schmitt over the last forty years. Starting from both the numerical and vehicular nature of (bank) money and endorsing Keynes's still unorthodox analysis on wage-units, it is indeed possible to provide a rigorous and logical explanation of the production-consumption process occurring in contemporary national economies. (Rossi, 1998, p. 10)

In these economies, income is defined as the exchange between two simultaneous emissions, one being monetary and the other real. This exchange, as with all other types of payments[15], concerns the same agent. This justifies the term 'absolute exchange,' adopted by Schmitt since 1966. This means that in a monetary production economy, the household is the only type of agent. As Schumpeter maintains (1934, p. 101), firms are simply intermediaries.

Production is a complex activity that turns into money income, which in turn transforms from two relative flows into the property of the same economic agent. Contrasting with the conventional, and currently accredited, economic theories, workers pay themselves. Through the intermediary bank, the worker transforms the real flow, represented by the heterogeneous results of work, into its uniform expression of monetary flow, in the form of a bank deposit.

Money income then has a concrete purchasing power because it is homologous of the total domestic product. The absolute exchange that occurs in production is therefore a macroeconomic operation, because money income, which naturally derives from production, is a positive supply for the national economy. "Money-income denotes the national output, and is therefore a real commodity, while a sum of money, taken as such, is a purely numerical and immaterial form" (Schmitt, 1996, p. 86-87).

Absolute exchange manifests in the market of factors of production. Through absolute exchange, newly produced goods—which are multiple and physically varied—gain a homogeneous numerical form

---

15   That is, those that occur in goods markets or financial markets.

that allows them to be measured in an economically coherent way. The payment of wages is then the only operation that can logically integrate money and output.

It can therefore be said that labor is the only factor of production, because the payment of wages defines collective income, or rather, the total cost of current output. National income is equivalent to the sum of wages earned, and the expenditure of income contributes, in part, to its redistribution.

This is highly plausible as the former statement relates to the factors of production market, whilst the latter refers to the product market, where consumer price affects income distribution, and therefore profit creation.

Capital accumulation and monetary pathologies

The following example based on Schmitt (1984) and Cencini (1985) is examined to further develop this explanation. It is assumed that by spending 100 (percent) of their income, workers purchase only 80 (percent) of current production.

The conclusion is simple.

By fixing sales prices at 125 (percent), firms gain a profit in the product market, thus acquiring a purchasing power that corresponds exactly with the amount of unsold goods (100 – 80 = 20). Monetary profit and its real content of 20 then come into existence. Let us imagine that in the following period the same firm invests the profit (20) and pays its workers who have produced the goods.

The product stands in for money and, because the product is purchased by the firm, the firm becomes the owner of fixed capital. At the same time, the workers gain the right to withdraw the stock realized in the preceding interval.

To summarize, the formation of fixed capital is a function of the investment of profit. It is easily accepted that income already invested (profit is an income)—and so transformed into fixed capital through the above procedure—can no longer be available in the financial market.

The purpose of a mono-departmental banking registration system incapable of logically describing and regulating accounting procedures then comes into question. This model inevitably assigns ownership of the fixed capital to the firm as a depersonified entity, giving the firm a sovereign status that further alienates workers. Furthermore, it is this process of capital accumulation that creates systemic socio-economic problems, including inflation and—in the long term—deflation, both of which generate unemployment.

On the other hand, a three-department accounting system would negate the original cause of the above scenario, or rather, it would allow income to be both transformed into capital and available for loan in the financial market. The banking structure should then be reformed as three technical-accounting departments, those being monetary, financial and capital.

The solution to the problem is then a change in the mechanics of accounting. Profit should be recorded in the financial department:

Diagram 1. Accounting record of profit in the 2nd department (financial)

2nd Dept. (financial)

Output *20*	Firm *20*

Diagram 1 illustrates the first accounting record of the profit of 20 realized by the example firm. The firm therefore becomes the holder of a deposit of the same sum in the financial department. Among the assets on the balance sheet we find the stock of unsold goods, which is the real content of the firm's income. If profit is invested, it transforms into capital. For accounting purposes, it is then necessary to move from the second to the third department:

Diagram 2. Amounts carried forward following the investment of profit from the 2nd department (financial) to the 3rd (fixed capital)

2nd Dept. (financial)		**3rd Dept. (fixed capital)**	
Output *20*	Firm *20*	2nd Dept. *20*	Firm *20*
Firm *20*	3rd Dept. *20*		

The new record in Diagram 2 presents the firm's corresponding property as fixed capital. The ledger represents the 'personified' firm, or the sum of all workers (units) working for the firm. The profit realized by the firm is then invested with the purpose of establishing capital for common enjoyment and use (more goods produced, better quality, lower costs).

For comparison, diagram 3 demonstrates what takes place in the introduction. Due to the monetary anomaly, the fixed capital is ascribed to the firm as a depersonalized entity. Due to the mixed accounts, the payment of wages is also registered, and overlaps with the investment of profit, in accordance with logic and the scenario depicted above.

Diagram 3. Mono-departmental accounting record

Single Dept.

Output *20*	Firm *20*
Firm *20*	Workers *20*

Capital in the third department should be correctly attributed in the records in diagram 2 to clarify the link between the material capital assets—physically present in the firm—and the manifestation of monetary capital in the accounts.

This is the key to understanding the natural economic connection between the 'personified' firm and capital. Without this transfer, profit is seemingly spent to purchase products. As the purchase is tied to the firm's core, workers are excluded from any economic entitlement regarding production.

Diagrams 4 and 5 configure the three-department system to register the payment of wages:

Diagram 4. Accounting records of the payment of wages in the 1st department (monetary)

1st Dept. (monetary)

Firm *20*	2nd Dept. *20*

Diagram 5. Amounts of the payment of wages carried forward to the 2nd department (financial)

2nd Dept. (financial)

1st Dept. 20	Workers 20

Both the first and second departments are balanced daily. At the end of the day[16], the first department has a balance of 0, with all income carried forward to the second department (diagram 6). The workers are holders of an income of 20 (or a deposit equal to 20), while the firm is a debtor of 20, which is registered in the financial department (diagram 7). Along with the transferred results of the third department, the second department is then balanced, and represents the profit contributed to the comprehensive macroeconomic order.

Diagram 6. The accounting epilogue at the end of the day in the 1st department (monetary) with the manifestation of income carried forward to the 2nd department (financial)

1st Dept. (monetary)		**2nd Dept. (financial)**	
Firm 20	2nd Dept. 20	1st Dept. 20	Workers 20
2nd Dept. 20	Firm 20	Firm 20	1st Dept. 20

Diagram 7. The accounting epilogue at the end of the day in the 2nd department (financial)

2nd Dept. (financial)

Firm 20	Workers 20

---

16   Banks produce closing reports daily: the calculation of interest is implemented the very next day.

Absolute exchange in the production-consumption process

The following procedure demonstrates that consumption is the effect of spending income in the product market. The presumption is that households are the (initial) owners of all newly produced goods and services the instant wages are paid. However, it is essential to distinguish between two types of consumption. Spending in the product market is a form of income distribution, since the physical goods are freed from the monetary form in which they were included *pro tempore* by income holders.

It is then necessary to reiterate that the payment of wages is *ipso facto* a creation, even though, in the case of investment of profit, it becomes an expenditure in the market of factors of production, the content of which is current output.

From a macroeconomic point of view, absolute exchange, which takes place in the quantum process of production, defines the economic consumption of newly produced goods, since the material result of labor is converted through the intermediary banking system into a certificate of deposit of equivalent value.

Newly produced goods lose their physical dimension when they are converted into money income; its purchasing power corresponds perfectly with the product itself. The income generated takes the form of a bank deposit and then gives the holder the right to withdraw on the national product for the same amount.

The payment of wages by firms and their (relative final) use by workers should be considered simultaneously. The first registration relates to the market of factors of production and represents the creation of national income.

The second registration is a result of spending income to purchase current output through the monetary intermediation of the banking system. The final act of purchasing current output by households can be considered a variation of absolute exchange. Through this exchange, workers replace their money income with real goods.

The monetary form representing units of purchasing power is dissolved, thus freeing its material content, or rather, the national product.

The formation of income and its distribution are therefore two opposite absolute exchanges. The first, which we might call the absolute positive exchange, defines the transformation of current output into money income, whereas the second, the absolute negative exchange, defines the transformation of income into physical products.

Recap

From this deliberation, we have deduced a strong link between the formation of inflation and unemployment and the absence of a well-regulated system of payments. However, such macroeconomic problems are not caused by agentic behavior, as neoclassical economists argue, but by the monetary and institutional anomalies related to the process of capital accumulation.

In this sense, the theory of money emissions differs from the endogenous growth theory[17], which underlines the microeconomic foundations of macroeconomics in mathematical representations of growth trajectories based on households maximizing utility and society maximizing profit.

The theory of money emissions is not a growth theory; it therefore does not deal with the economic impacts of innovation, technological change, human capital and spillover effects.

Schmitt's real contribution to our understanding of the accumulation of capital is his analysis of profits. He maintains that profits in the current model are duplicated artificially during the process of income creation to generate a deposit that will never run out.

---

17   Cf. Solow (1956).

APPLICATIONS IN MICROCREDIT

Quantum credit and ordinary credit

As stated above, the payment of wages is the macroeconomic action *par excellence*.

As the means for the payment of wages, the real product is assigned a numerical form in cash money. The payment of wages therefore leads to an income that increases the wealth of a given economic system. As Cencini and Borghi (2010) observe, economic production is not physical creation but monetary creation, and income is the link between money and output.

From a quantum economic point of view, output is an instant event that coincides with the payment of wages. This income is defined as macroeconomic precisely because it influences the evolution of the system, increasing the endogenous economic substance.

It is therefore not a question that can be resolved on a purely numeric level.

Whether the action is limited to a single agent or extends to the systemic level, the fact that production generally adds wealth does not change. Wages are financed by the very workers for whom they are intended. The income they receive does not come from an outside source.

The *poìesis* is instantaneous and concurrent with the moment workers are accredited. If the payment of wages occurs through intermediary banks (operating costs are overlooked for the sake of example), it is easy to observe how the concession of credit to the firm for remuneration comes from its workers whose production activities are the firm's only source of income.

These credit operations are quantum in nature.

Through the three-departmental accounting registration system, opening a line of credit[18] to pay wages is not compromised *a priori*—

---

18   The use of bank notes, on the contrary, due to their conventional character, requires the supplying institution to have a debit with the issuing

not even in cases of microcredit. The level of poverty of the aspiring entrepreneur would then be irrelevant, and a request for peremptory protective guarantee unreasonable. In effect—*mutando orationem aliis verbis*—no initial capital is necessary as it is the payment of wages that generates the necessary income to repay the conceded credit. Income is created by output and, in an economic sense, it also defines the product.

By lending wage income to firms, banks allow them to invest it, thus transforming output into stock. The debt entry of a microenterprise finds its equivalent counterpart in assets, composed of the stock of real goods.

Financing to invest in plants and machinery, fixed assets of various kinds (patents, licenses, etc.) and raw materials necessary for material production—or rather the physical transformation of components and energy—inevitably requires spending previously acquired income. It is then a clear case of consumer financing and, as such, of ordinary bank credit operations.

Intermediary institutions must therefore preemptively gather the resources required to grant loans. Ordinary bank credit then inescapably derives from precedent quantum credit, although this position is logical and not chronological. Banks can easily alternate between ordinary and quantum credit in their business activities by adjusting double-entry bookkeeping mechanisms used to balance their accounts.

Financing credit for consumption does not create or destroy new units of wealth; it is merely a transfer of income from one constituent to another. With no macro repercussions, these credit operations are clearly microeconomic activities. However, the true meaning of consumption has clear macroeconomic repercussions.

Consumption makes it possible to properly define the typical money circuit, which begins with production[19]. A model in which workers purchase a part of the goods produced by themselves from

---

central bank (or rather, on a second level, with the clients who possess them), thus increasing the complexity of the relationship.

19 When this does not happen, that is, when stock is left unsold—the firm is missing the equivalent amount of income—the firm's capacity to pay off its debt with the bank diminishes. The accounts remain in balance due to the credit owed to the workers by the firm (and if interests are paid regularly by the firm, there should be no inconvenience for the institution), but the risk of prolonging this condition is that it leads to the precarious situation becoming definitive.

their own firm (beneficiary of a quantum credit) results in a reduction of their credit with the bank. This is immediately balanced by an equal decrease in the debit that the firm has with the lending institution. The purchase of output takes away part of the wage income in its numerical form, which it receives at the moment of payment. Money, no longer having real content, loses the purchasing power bestowed on it by production.

According to Cencini and Borghi (2010), consumption means to take possession of a physical product, which then strips it of the monetary form given in production. Due to consumption, a destruction of income equal to the value of products purchased occurs.

Up to this point, the argument has been extremely simplified with a model consisting of a bank, a firm and its workers. Nevertheless, even on a larger scale, the above balances are always retained in accounting—even against the greater complexities of the real system, in which various banks interact with an array of firms and the workers linked to them.

What is identified is a more articulate set of records that necessarily considers interrelations and interbank relationships. This can be extrapolated from the hypothetical situation in which a firm (or various firms) is unable to sell part of its stock. The interrelations and interdependence of the described model would then determine the continuation of debt, no longer between the institution and workers (the implicit financers of the firm), but between banks, which would certainly be less desirable for them.

Even in a situation where the microentrepreneur is also the sole worker of the firm, the described dynamics do not change. On a formal level, the distinct phases between the objective aspect (the firm) and the subjective aspect (labor and production) simply happen to manifest in the same entity.

The socioeconomic sustainability of microcredit

Literature on microcredit often discusses the necessity for crediting institutions to implement strenuous resource procurement strategies and to outline tools for the mitigation of credit risk.

The following monetary analysis on commercial financing for production demonstrates that neither of the aforementioned issues are of concern. As it stands, lending does not directly affect income creation. Income is generated exclusively by the labor of the microentrepreneur and/or their business partners, who indirectly finance themselves.

The microfinancing entity (either directly or indirectly through a connected institution) only needs to help pay wages ahead of time, which does not modify the fundamental nature of the described model.

The threats faced by the institution supplying ordinary bank credit are addressed below.

A possible threat arises in the case of unsold stock, although, support and monitoring techniques of specialized microcredit agents—assisted by planning and sales systems—have reduced these occurrences and their troublesome degeneration considerably. Guarantee funds, reinsurance and portfolio protection investments are also applied to further reduce the weight of discontinuity, should it manifest. The sale of the company's securities (stocks and bonds) is particularly pertinent for obtaining the capital necessary to finance these measures, and constitute a productive reinvestment of the income lent. The demand for specific tools and special investment funds in ethical and sustainability microfinance projects is also particularly high. The current supply[20] barely covers 4% of demand, leaving various areas open for funding. Indubitably, microfinance institutions should strive to gather endogenous savings, and reach operative—as well as financial—self-sufficiency; this being particularly advisable for mutual organizations, cooperatives and consortiums.

In addition to the above, we should consider the positive effects of a strategy that modulates the depth of outreach of credit operations such that recipient firms can sustainably transfer resources to cover larger costs (and defer risk). A further desirable foundation for the model is government intervention to stimulate and regulate access to microcredit, in line with universal constitutional laws that protect Human dignity[21].

We would then have a system characterized by perfected financial inclusion with minimal risk for the supplying institutions, clear social benefits, generalized monetary order and positive macroeconomic

---

20   Cf. Cencini and Borghi, 2010, p. 100.
21   Cf. Borghi (2010).

manifestations. Relieved of the heavy welfare load, the government could free a great portion of its resources currently dedicated to subsidies (and therefore included in current spending), and would be able to fulfill its constitutional duties and virtuous efforts as a guarantor more effectively.

REFERENCES

Altman, E. I. (1993). *Corporate financial distress and bankruptcy: A complete guide to predicting & avoiding distress and profiting from bankruptcy* (2nd ed.). New York: John Wiley & Sons.

Bachelier, L. (1900). *Théorie de la spéculation*. Paris: Gauthier-Villars.

Basel Committee on Banking Supervision, & Bank for International Settlements (2004). *International convergence of capital measurement and capital standards: A revised framework*. Basel, Switzerland: Bank for International Settlements.

Beaver, W.H., Correia, M., & McNichols, M.F. (2010). Financial statement analysis and the prediction of financial distress. *Foundations and Trends in Accounting, 5*(2), 99-173.

Bertuglia, C.S., & Vaio, F. (2005). *Nonlinearity, chaos and complexity: The dynamics of natural and social systems*. Oxford: Oxford University Press.

Brown, R. (1828). A brief account of microscopical observations made in the months of June, July and August 1827, on the particles contained in the pollen of plants; and on the general existence of active molecules in organic and inorganic bodies. *The Philosophical Magazine, 4*(21), 161-173.

Capiński, M., & Zastawniak, T. (2003). *Mathematics for finance: An introduction to financial engineering*. London: Springer.

Cencini, A. (1982). The logical indeterminacy of relative prices. In M. Baranzini (Ed.), *Advances in economic theory* (pp. 126-137). Oxford and New York: Basil Blackwell and St. Martin's Press.

Cencini, A. (1984). *Time and the macroeconomic analysis of income*. London and New York: Pinter Publishers.

Cencini, A. (1985). Production circulaire, échange et théorie quantique. In B. Schmitt (Ed.), *Production et monnaie* (pp. 83-94). Paris: Sirey.

Cencini, A. (1988). *Money, income and time, with a preface by Meghnad Desai*. London and New York: Pinter Publishers.

Cencini, A. (1997). *Monetary theory. National and international* (pbk ed.). London and New York: Routledge.

Cencini, A. (2001). *Monetary macroeconomics. A new approach*. London and New York: Routledge.

Cencini, A. (2005). *Macroeconomic foundations of macroeconomics*. London and New York: Routledge.

Cencini, A. (2008). *Elementi di Macroeconomia monetaria*. Padova: CEDAM.

Cencini, A., & Borghi, M. (2010). *Per un contributo allo sviluppo del microcredito*. Padova: CEDAM.

Clower, R.W. (1977). The anatomy of monetary theory. *The American Economic Review, 67*(1), 206-212.

Damodaran, A. (2015). *Applied corporate finance*. Hoboken, NJ: John Wiley & Sons.

Danovi, A., & Quagli, A. (2010). *Crisi aziendali e processi di risanamento: Previsione e diagnosi, terapie, casi aziendali*. Milano: IPSOA.

Duffie, D., & Singleton K.J. (2003). *Credit risk: Pricing, measurement, and management*. Princeton, NJ: Princeton University Press.

Fisher, R. (1936). The use of multiple measurements in taxonomic problems. *Annals of Eugenics, 7*(2), 179-188.

Gallager, R.G. (2013). *Stochastic processes: Theory for applications*. Cambridge: Cambridge University Press.

Goldstein, J.A., Mininni, R.M., & Romanelli S. (2007). Markov semigroups and estimating functions, with applications to some financial models. *Communications on Stochastic Analysis, 1*, 3, 343-355.

Graziani, A. (1989). *The theory of the monetary circuit* (Thames Papers in Political Economy No. 1). London: Thames Polytechnic.

Hoek, J., & Elliott, R.J. (2012). Asset pricing using finite state markov chain stochastic discount functions. *Stochastic Analysis and Applications, 30*, 865-894.

Isaacson, D., & Madsen, R. (1985). *Markov chains: Theory and applications*. Malabar, FL: R.E. Krieger Publishing Company.

Israel, R.B., Rosenthal, J.S., & Wei, J.Z. (2001). Finding generators for Markov chains via empirical transition matrices, with applications to credit ratings. *Mathematical Finance, 11*, 245-265.

Jarrow, R.A., Lando, D., & Turnbull, S. (1997). A Markov model for term structure of credit risk spreads. *Review of Financial Studies, 10*, 481-523.

Keynes, J.M. (1930). *A Treatise on Money* (Vols. 1-2). London: Macmillan.

Keynes, J.M. (1973a). A Monetary Theory of Production. In E. Johnson & D. Moggridge (Eds.), *The collected writings of John Maynard Keynes: Volume 13* (pp. 408-411). London: Macmillan. (Original work published 1933)

Keynes, J.M. (1973b). *The collected writings of John Maynard Keynes: Volume 7*. London: Macmillan.

Knight, F.H. (1967). Laissez-faire: Pro and con. *Journal of Political Economy, 75*, 782-795.

Marx, K. (1859). *A contribution to the critique of political economy*. Berlin: Franz Duncker.

Marx, K. (1973). *Grundrisse*. Harmondsworth: Penguin. (Original work published 1939)

Meyn, S.P., & Tweedie, R.L. (1993). *Markov chains and stochastic stability*.

London: Springer.

Migliori, S. (2013). *Crisi d'impresa e corporate governance.* Milano: FrancoAngeli.

Negri, I. (2004). Appunti del corso di modelli stocastici e analisi dei sati. Bergamo: CELSB.

Pilkington, M. (2010). Transnational corporations in a global monetary theory of production: A world-systems perspective. *Journal of World-Systems Research, 16,* 246-265.

Ricardo, D. (1951). *On the principles of political economy and taxation.* Cambridge: Cambridge University Press. (Original work published 1817)

Rossi, S. (1998). Endogenous money and banking activity: Some notes on the workings of modern payment systems. *Studi Economici, 53,* 23-56.

Rossi, S. (2006). The theory of money emissions. In P. Arestis & M.C. Sawyer (Eds.), *A handbook of alternative monetary economics* (pp. 121-138). Cheltenham, UK: Edward Elgar.

Salsa, S. (2010). *Equazioni a derivate parziali: Metodi, modelli e applicazioni.* Milano: Springer.

Schmitt, B. (1966). *Monnaie, salaires et profits.* Paris: Presses Universitaires de France.

Schmitt, B. (1972). *Macroeconomic theory: A fundamental revision.* Albeuve: Castella.

Schmitt, B. (1984). *Inflation, chômage et malformations du capital: Macroéconomie quantique.* Paris et Albeuve: Economica et Castella.

Schmitt, B. (1985). Un nouvel ordre monétaire international: Le plan Keynes. In F. Poulon et al. (Eds.), *Les écrits de Keynes* (pp. 195-209). Paris: Dunod.

Schmitt, B. (1996). A new paradigm for the determination of money prices. In G. Deleplace & E.J. Nell (Eds.), *Money in motion: The post Keynesian and circulation approaches* (pp. 105-138). New York: Macmillan and St. Martin's Press.

Schumpeter, J.A. (1934). *The theory of economic development.* Cambridge, MA: Harvard University Press.

Sericola, B. (2013). *Markov chains: Theory, algorithms and applications.* London: ISTE Ltd.

Smith, A. (1976). *An inquiry into the nature and causes of the wealth of nations.* New York: Oxford University Press. (Originally published 1776)

Solow, R.M. (1956). A contribution to the theory of economic growth. *The Quarterly Journal of Economics, 70*(1), 65-94.

Starr, R. M. (1989). *General equilibrium models of monetary economies: Studies in the static foundations of monetary theory.* Boston: Academic Press (Harcourt Brace Jovanovich).

Venturi, B., & Casula, G. (2014). *Fondamenti di matematica per le scienze economiche, aziendali e finanziarie.* Roma: Aracne.

Venturi, B., & Casula, G. (2014). *Lecture notes in Mathematics.* University of Cagliari.

Walras, L. (1952). *Eléments d'économie politique pure; ou, la théorie de la richesse sociale.* Paris: Librairie Generale de Droit et de Jurisprudence. (Original work published 1874)

Walras, L. (1954). *Elements of pure economics; or, the theory of social wealth* (W. Jaffé, Trans.). London: George Allen & Unwin Ltd. (Original work published 1874)

Wicksell, J.G.K. (1903). *Den dunkla punkten i penningteorien och En lektion i banklagstiftning.* Stockholm.

Yun, J. (2011). *A present-value approach to variable selection.* University of Chicago Booth School of Business.

Zappa, G. (1946). *Il reddito di impresa: Scritture doppie, conti e bilanci di aziende commerciali* (2nd ed.). Milano: Giuffrè.

OTHER ANAPHORA LITERARY PRESS TITLES

The History of British and American Author-Publishers
By: Anna Faktorovich

Notes for Further Research
By: Molly Kirschner

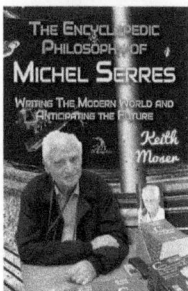

The Encyclopedic Philosophy of Michel Serres
By: Keith Moser

The Visit
By: Michael G. Casey

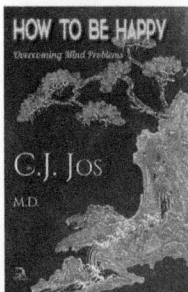

How to Be Happy
By: C. J. Jos

A Dying Breed
By: Scott Duff

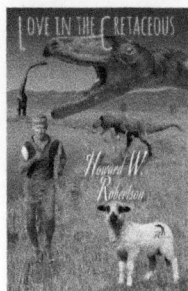

Love in the Cretaceous
By: Howard W. Robertson

The Second of Seven
By: Jeremie Guy